BUTCH'S RULES

The Book of Philosophical Rules
And Suggestions For Better living!

Author Warren (Butch) Thompson, Jr.

Dedication

This book is dedicated to anyone who endeavors to pursue critical thinking of things big and small, and challenge conventional wisdom, which may be correct or incorrect. This book suggest that there is always a better way of doing things and a better way to make decisions about everything.

PREFACE

This book is dedicated to the principle that there is always a better way to do anything, or improve on your previous decisions. Whether it is the question of learning to manage your money better or deciding about choosing the best job, or career, to pursue, this book has a "take-a-way" piece of advise to help you in making better decisions. At he end of the day, what will help you is the learning to be a better critical thinker, or learn to apply critical thinking, to any task, or situation you may encounter. As technology and science offers us better and fast ways to do everything, then learning to think, and problem solve, better with improve your (our) decision making process, and, thereby, improve your (our) lives. This book offers the results of my attempt to think more deeply about basic ideas, and beliefs, and misconception, and the opportunity to revisit all of your (our) past, present and future decisions. I believe that there is not always a better way and best decision available.

Table of Contents

35 Butch's Rules

Butch's Rule #1 - Self-Empowerment

Butch's Rule #2 - Better Decision Making Formula

Butch's Rule #3 - Positive People

Butch's Rule #4 - When All Else Fails, Read The Instructions

Butch's Rule #5 - Become A Life Long Saver

Butch's Rule #6 - Common Sense

Butch's Rule #7 - Never Blame The Victim

Butch's Rule #8 - Be The Better Person

Butch's Rule #9 - Pursuing Success

Butch's Rule #10 - Practice Makes Better

Butch's Rule #11 - The Money Rule

Butch's Rule #12 - The Multi-Tasking Rule

Butch's Rule #13 - The Truth Always Wins Out In The End

Butch's Rule #14 - The Career Choice Rule

Butch's Rule #15 - Pursuing Your Dreams

Butch's Rule #16 - The Wealth Building Rule

Butch's Rule #17 - Actions Speak Louder Then Words

Butch's Rule #18 - The Golden Rule

Butch's Rule #19 - The Family Rule

Butch's Rule #20 - Honesty Is The Best Policy

Butch's Rule #21 - Both Winning and Losing Can Teach You Lessons

Butch's Rule #22 - It's Always Better To Be Tolerant and Accepting of Other People

Butch's Rule #23 - Always Be Supportive of Education

Butch's Rule #24 - The Best Answer Rule

Butch's Rule #25 - The Programming Yourself for Success Rule
Butch's Rule #26 - The Psychology of Success Rule

Butch's Rule #27 - The Dating and Mating Rule

Butch's Rule #28 - Always Re-Confirm 2nd Hand Information Rule

Butch's Rule #29 - It Is Better To Be Positive Rule

Butch's Rule #30 - If you want a better future, you have to do something different, and better, than you have done in the past.

Butch's Rule #31 - Always Practice Good Manners

Butch's Rule #32 - The Anti-Discrimination Rule

Butch's Rule #33 - National Healthcare is a Pact

Butch's Rule #34 - The Employee Mutual Company (EMC)

Butch's Rule #35 - It's Better to be a Reader than a Non-Reader

Butch's Rule #1

Self-Empowerment

People always wonder why they are in the place, in their lives, that they are. Well, for the most part, where you are is in large part based on many of the decisions you have made in the past to bring you to where you are. If you change the way you make decisions, you can change your life. This is the thesis of this book. It is not all chance that places you were you are. You have more control and power then you might want to admit, or understand. Most people think that fate, or destiny, placed them where they are. The truth is that there are a multitude of conscious decisions which contributed to where you are in your life today. Again, You have the power to change the way you make decisions, and change your life.

Short Illustrations:

After Losing her job, Sarah decided she wouldn't wait for a recruiter to call. She recognized her past decision to only network passively had contributed to her current situation. She took controll by immediately enrolling in a certification course and proactively reaching out to 20 industry contacts a week.

Butch's Rule #2

Better Decision Making Formula

Learning to make better decisions can improve the quality and direction of your life. A simple formula to do so would be to imagine there are at least two options to chose from with every major decision you have to make. Learn to carefully analyze the ramifications of the two options, then chose the one that is better based on all available information. This exercise over time will help to make you a stronger, better decision maker.

Short Illustration:

Before buy a new car, Tom faced two options: (A) A brand-new expensive SUV with high monthly payments, or (B) A two-year-old reliable sedan with lower monthly payments and a proven maintenance history. He analyzed the ramifications (saving less vs saving more) and chose (B) to better align with his long-term financial goals.

Butch's Rule #3

Positive People

Always surround yourself with positive people. There are people who are positive influences in your life, and there are people who have a negative influences in your life. You have control over who you spend your time with and who you let into your life.

Short Illustration:

Mark started avoiding his college friend, David, who constainly complained about their mutual workplace, discouraged Mark's career ideas, and rarely celebrated his successes. Instead, Mark began spending more time with his colleague, Lisa, who was always brainstorming new projects and offering encouraging advice, thereby surrounding himself with a positive influencer.

Butch's Rule #4

When All Else Fails, Read The Instructions.

When all else fails, read the instructions. There are instructions and books available to help you understand, and do, most things you might wish to do. If you have questions, you will always do better when you read available information for most of your answers. This is why the internet is so popular, because of the easily availability helpful information. Though, it is always good, to have your own personal library of reference books and materials available, when all else fails, or before all else fails, read the instructions.

Short Illustration:

Trying to assemble a new piece of furniture, Maria became frustrated when the legs wouldn't attach. Before throwing the whole thing across the room, she finally opened the manual (the instructions), realizing she was using the short bolts instead of the lone one for the step.

Butch's Rule #5

Become A Life Long Saver

Learn to be a saver: There is no decision that you can make that will be smarter for your present and future, then learning to be a life long saver.

Short Illustration:

Starting with his first paycheck, David committed to automatically transfering 10% of his income into a savings account before he paid any bill. This habit of being a life-long saver ensured that 20 years later, he had a significant emergency fund and the down payment for a house.

Butch's Rule #6

Common Sense

Good is Good, and Bad is Bad.

Short Illustrations:

Jane saw a co-worker stealing office supplies. Applying commonse, she immeditaly understood that stealing is bad and reporting it was the right thing to do for the company's well-being and her own integrity, even though it was an uncomfortable situation.

Butch's Rule #7

Never Blame The Victim

Never blame the victim. The guilty party is always the party that perpetrated the original sin.

Short Illustration:

A woman's apartment broken into. Some neighbors suggest that she should have better security or been more careful. Applying this rule, Detecdtive Miller quickly dismissed those suggestions, stating the guilty party is always the one who perpetrated the crime, focusing his investigation solely on the burglar.

Butch's Rule #8

Be The Better Person

<u>Truism:</u> In every person's life, we all have moments where we run into "forks in the road". These are times, or places, or moments, where we have to make a very important decision whether we will choose, or decide, one way or another, one direction, or another, left or right, up or down. When we have to make an important decision as to which way we will choose, it is a truism that when you are at one of these major "forks in the road", it is always better to take the high road, versus the low road.

Short Illustration:

During a heated professional meeting, a rival colleague made a disrepectful personal jab at Sarah. Instead of retaliating with an equally harsh insult (the low road), Sarah chose to take the high road by calmly addressing the business point, showing superior professionalism,and restain.

Butch's Rule #9

Pursuing Success

In the study of what makes a person, project, or company, successful, it can be concluded that success is not guaranteed, but, no matter the proposed idea, or project, there is no doubt that you can always guarantee the efforts you put forth in helping to make the project a more successful one. With consistent best efforts in everything that you do, you will always increase the probability that you will always be more successful, then unsuccessful. Make it a rule that you always put forth your best efforts, always doing a job that, whether you win or lose, you can be proud of. The difference in winning and losing may directly depend on the effort you put forth.

Short Illustration:

While launching his startup, Micheal worked tirelessly, putting in 14 hour days to refine his product and secure funding. He recognized that market success wasn't guaranteed. He could always guarantee his best efforts. His consistent high quality work significantly increased his company's probability of success.

Butch's Rule #10

Practice Makes Better

Practice does not make perfect: It is practice that makes you better, and, with practice, you can always get better today then you were yesterday. The person who works at their craft everyday will always be better then the person who doesn't. You are what you do everyday, and over time.

Short Illustration:

A musician, Anna, played her violin for at least an hour every single day. She understand that she wouldn't achieve "perfect", but though this daily, consistent practice, she found that she was better today than she was yesterday, constantly improving her technique and repertoire.

Butch's Rule #11

The Money Rule

<u>The Money Rule</u>: If you have the regular habit of spending more than you make, you will become poorer and poorer. If you have the regular habit of spending less than you make, you will become richer and richer. It is under your control to choose which habit to follow.

Short Illustration:

Lisa makes $5,000 per month. She realized that by spending onlu $4,000 each month (spending less than she makes), she was able to invest the extra $1,000, actively toward becoming richer. If she spent $5,000 and acrueddebt, she would be following the habit that leads to becoming poorer.

Butch's Rule #12

The Multi-Tasking Rule

Multi-tasking: When you multi-task, you are only dividing your attention between multiple tasks, and giving each of the tasks only a fraction of your attention. When there is a task which requires your undivided full attention give it your undivided full attention. There are some tasks that are so important that a distracted error could prove to be very costly. The questions is: How many eggs can you juggle without breaking one?

Short Illustration:

While driving on a busy highway, John got a text message. He knew that reading and responding would divide his attention and an error could be costly. He chose to give the task of driving his undivided attention and wait until he was safely parked to check his phone.

Butch's Rule #13

The Truth Always Wins Out In The End.

Always remember, that the truth, what is right, correct, and honorable, always wins in the end. It is always better to be as truthful as possible in all your personal and professional dealings. Because when examined, the truth always holds up, and the truth never changes.

Short Illustration:

When questioned by his supervisor about a failed project, Mark considered bending the facts to shift blame, he chose to be as truthful as possible, laying out the facts as they happened. This honesty held up under scrutiny, providng that the truth always wins out and preserved his reputation.

Butch's Rule #14

The Career Choice Rule

One of the smartest, and most fulfilling, things anyone can do, as early in life as possible, is to find work, or a pursuit, that they enjoy doing. In the case of work, for the average person, a career, or work life, can last 30, 40, 50, 60, or more years. Therefore, if a person can find work that they enjoy, as early in life as possible, the happier they might be in their working life, and in their pursuit of happiness in their life, in general. Nothing could be worst then doing something for 30, 40, 50, 60 or more years, that a person does not enjoy doing, or work or job that a person is unhappy doing.

Short Illustration:

Sarah turned down a high-paying job in finance to become a teacher because she genuinely enjoyed the process of mentoring students. She recognize that since her work life would last decades, choosing a pursuit she enjoyed doing would lead to greater happiness than simply chasing the largest salary.

Butch's Rule #15

Pursuing Your Dreams

When you are pursuing your dreams, don't get discouraged when you do not get all the support, or encouragement, that you think you should get from others. Most people can not see how important your dream is to you, but those same people will be among the first to congratulate you when you succeed. All you really need is the belief in yourself, and that you can fulfill your dreams.

Short Illustration:

When James decided to quit his corporate job to start a bakery, his relatives express strong doubts and lack of support. Instead of getting discouraged, James focused on his belief in himself and his business plan, knowing that once he succeeded those same people would be the first to congratulate him.

Butch's Rule #16

The Wealth Building Rule

True wealth is not measured by income, but by net worth. It's not measured by what you make, but what you keep. It is more important to grow your net worth, then to grow your income. Though, if you have increasing income, increasing income can provide the opportunity to help increase your net worth.

Short Illustration:

A doctor earned $1,250.000 has a net worth of $50,000. A small business owner earns $75,000 has a net worth of $500,000. The small business owner has greater wealth because he focused on growing his net worth (what he kept and invested), not just his income (what he made).

Butch's Rule #17

Actions Speak Louder Words

There is no such thing as a mixed-message. There is no such thing as "do as I say, and not as I do". The logically conclusion, or deduction, following a "mixed-message", is that your actions will always speak louder then your words". If your actions are contrary to your words, what is called "incongruence", then the dominate message received is from your actions. Your actions will always over-ride your verbal message. It is what you do, your non-verbal message, that is the much stronger message communicated.

Short Illustration:

A politician constantly gave speeches about the importance of reducing carbon emissions but constantly flew on private jets for short trips. The public saw his actions (the private jet use) as the dominate message of his true priorities, overriding his verbal commitment (the speeches).

Butch's Rule #18

The Golden Rule

Remember to practice "The Golden Rule" in how you treat others. "One should treat others as one would like others to treat oneself ". Though, you may not be able to imagine it today, you may need another person's help, or assistance, one day. Whether you are young, old, rich, poor, healthy, or live with some limitations, you may need the help, and kindness, of another in the future. If you were to judge yourself today based on how you treat others, would you judge yourself favorably. If you had a twin, a soul-mate, someone just like yourself, would that person answer your call for help, or assistance. Your answer to that question I hope is "Yes", that person would be there for me. He, or she, is a person of kindness, and one who would be there for me in my time of need. Always treat others the way you wish to be treated.

Short Illustration:

When a new, shy intern joined the company, senior employee Alex made a point to introduce himself, offering help, and including the intern to lunch invitations. Alex was simply treating others as he would like to be treated, anticipating that one day he might be the person needing a little kindness and support.

Butch's Rule #19

The Family Rule

From one generation to the next, you will forever be connected to your parents, and your children. Whatever your parents gave you to help you to enjoy your life, you should be willing to share with your parents, in return, to support them in their latter years. You will never know all the sacrifices and events that occurred before you arrived to bring you into the life you enjoy, which is the total biography of your parents, and, in turn, their should be no limit as to what you are willing to do to help your children to have a good life. Again, you will always be connected like links of a chain to your parents and children forever thru time. Your parents are forever a part of your family history, and your children are forever a part of your legacy, present and future.

Short Illustration:

As her family aged, Maria used some of savings and time to help them with home maintenance and daily care, understanding it was her turn to share with her parents in return for all they had done. She simutaneously prioritied paying for her children's college education, and solidifying her role as a link in the family chain.

Butch's Rule #20

Honesty Is The Best Policy

It's true that "Honesty is the best policy". Though, there are probably few people who are 100% honest 100% of the time, it is better to be more honest then not. The truth will not only set you free, but it also resolves most problems sooner rather then later. You will always earn invaluable respect universally, versus universal scorn for being dishonest. If you get caught not being honest, do the right thing, quickly apologize, learn from the episode, and learn to be more honest in the future, and a better person. You can always learn to be a better person today then the person you were before, and most people will respect you for it.

Short Illustration:

A restaurant server accidentally overcharged a customer b $5.00. Instead of hoping the customer wouldn't notice, the server immediately admitted the mistake, apologized, and quickly corrected the bill. The customer appreciated the honesty and left a large tip, showing the invaluable respect earned by being truthful.

Butch's Rule #21

Both Winning and Losing Can Teach You Lessons

If you lose, the lesson is that you need to make a change. If you win, the lesson is there is something you need to learn and repeat. In other words, every experience is a learning experience. It is up to you to figure out the important lesson being revealed to you. In the study of the secret to being successful, learning to be successful is about learning from success, and failure. As it is said "Success (and failure) leaves clues.

Short Illustration:

When a company's new product launch failed (losing) , the team analyzed their market research and found it was flawed, learned that they need to make a change in strategy. When the subsequent product succeeded (winning), they documented the successful marketing tactics to learn and repeat them.

Butch's Rule #22

It's Always Better To Be Tolerant and Accepting of Other People

It is always better to be tolerant and accepting of others, then to be intolerant and un-accepting of others. Remember, if you are anti-other people, then you are also projecting that it is acceptable for others to be un-accepting of you, and your perceived differences. It is better to work together as one people, then to fight separately as many other people. Together we are stronger, and divided we are weak. It is better to have more friends, then to create enemies of other's perceived differences. Again, it is always better to be tolerant and accepting of all other people.

Short Illustration:

In a diverse neighborhood, a new resident with a different cultural background moved in. Instead of viewing the difference negatively, the existing community member chose to be tolerant and accepting, organizing a potlock to learn about the resident's culture, believing that working together as one people made the community stronger.

Butch's Rule #23

Always Be Supportive of Education

Whether it is your own education, or your children's education, your friend's education, your neighbor's education, your community's education, or any educational institution, it is, and will always be, an enriching experience, and one that is value added. The person who pursues the acquisition of a better, and higher, education is the person who qualitatively puts themselves on a path to improve their life.

Generally speaking, by definition, education is the process of facilitating learning, and, it goes without saying, that those who are more educated make more money, have better employment prospects, travel more, contribute to their communities more, are more articulate, more literate, and, overall, have better lives. This is why successful people strive to make sure their children have the best education possible to help to insure that they have a better chance at success in their lives.

Short Illustration:

Even though she was busy raising a family, Susan dedicated each week to volunteer as a reading tutor at her local public school. She was supportive of education by facilitation learning for others, believing that the pursuit of a better education puts people on the path to improving their lives.

Butch's Rule #24

The Best Answer Rule

The best answer to a negative is a positive. When something bad happens, the best answer is the most positive remedy. The best response to unfairness is fairness. The best response to failure is success. The best answer to what is wrong will always be what is right. Learning to do things the right way is always the best response to doing things the wrong way.

Short Illustration:

After receiving a harsh and unfair criticism from a client (a negative). the marketing team's leader didn't retaliate. Instead, he crafted a professional, detailed response outlining how they would fix the problem and exceed expectations (a positive remedy). He chose the most positive remedy as the best answer to the negative.

Butch's Rule #25

The Programming Yourself for Success Rule

It is a well known fact that you physically get what you think about most. This is why it is always good to be goal oriented, and, at times, single-minded in what you want. Success programming is no more then having a goal and focusing on it until it has been accomplished. What you think about most is what you get. You, me, anyone can program themselves to be more successful.

Short Illustration:

Jennifer wanted to run a marathon. She created a detailed training schedule and every morning, she would visualize herself across the finish line, strong and healthy. By being goal oriented and constantly focusing on it, she was programming herself for success, making the physical accomplishment lore likely.

Butch's Rule #26

The Psychology of Success Rule

The psychology of success is the belief that you can win, or succeed, before you have done so. The truth is that it can be a bigger psychological hurdle then just saying the words "I believe that I can win, or do this task that I have never done before". It is probably a mixture of believe that you can accomplish the yet to be accomplished, and breaking thru the limiting fear, which we all have to a degree. Fear sometimes it is rational, and sometimes irrational, but we should always challenge fears which appear irrational, or not base on the reality, or empirical, evidence. If a task has been done before by a statistically significant number of people, then, logically, there is no rational reason why you should not be able to accomplish the same task successfully. Obviously, there is no guaranteed of success with any task, but the probably of success, if the task has been done many times before by multiple examples, should give you confidence that it is not an insurmountable venture, or task, to undertake.

Short Illustration:

Imagine facing a high mountain you've never climed before. Fear calls it impossible, but a worn trail proves thousands have reached the peak. By replacing ration doubt with the empirical evidence of others' success, you gain the ng th to climb, winning the mental battle before taking the first step

Butch's Rule #27

The Dating and Mating Rule

If you are looking for someone to have fun with, then go for beauty. If you are looking for someone to spend time with, then I would advise choosing someone with the most pleasant personality. Obviously, most people would like to have both, the best of both characteristics, someone with beauty and a pleasant personality, but, If you had to choose one characteristic over the other, for the long run, then it is advisable to chose a partner with a pleasant personality over a partner which may be more beautiful. This rule works whether you are male, or female. Again, if you are trying to decide which would be the better decision, or choice, I advice you go for someone with a more pleasant personality.

Short Illustration:

Micheal met two women: one who was strikingly beautiful but often moody and demanding, and another who was pleasant, kind, and always uplifting to be around. For a long-term partner, he decided to choose the one with the pleasant personality over mere beauty, believing that kind would make for a happier life together.

Butch's Rule #28

Always Re-Confirm 2nd Hand Information Rule

Whether it is business, personal, political, social or informal gossip, you should always reconfirm any second hand news or information, particularly if the information is going to be used to be part of an important decision making process. If you have to make an important decision, whether business, personal, political or social, you don't want to come to an incorrect conclusion base on the acceptance and use of incorrect information. As it is said in the business world, garbage in, garbage out. The more correct, or precise, the information you use to make important decision, the more likely you will make a better decision.

Short Illustration:

Sarah hearn office gossip that her department was going to be downsized. Before updating her resume and panicking (an important decision), she went directly to her manager (a primary source) to re-confirm the second-hand information. She discovered the rumor was false and only a small team was being restructured.

Butch's Rule #29

It Is Better To Be Positive Rule

If you start your day off in a positive mood, or frame of mind, you are more likely to end your day in a positive mood, or frame of mind. It is better to look at your glass as half full, versus being half empty, because it really is. In closing, always remember that it is a truism that you will always accomplish more being positive then you ever will being negative.

Short Illustration:

When faced with a challenging week of deadlines, Mark chose to view it as an exciting opportunity to show case his skills (glass half full) rather than an overwhelming burden (glass half empty). This positive frame of mind helped him stay focused and energetic, enabling him to accomplish more.

Butch's Rule #30

If you want a better future, you have to do some-

thing different, and better, than you have done in the past.

If you want a better future, you have do to something different, and better, then you have done in the past. If you want positive change, you have to change in a more positive and affirmative direction (s). Change is inevitable, and is always happening, whether we want it to or not, it is up to you, and within your power, to influence what that change can be.

Short Illustration:

A business consistently missed it's quarterly sales goals. The owner recognized that doing the same old pitches wouldn't change the outcome. To create a better future the company changed in a more positive affirmative direction by completely restructuring the sales process and adopting new technology.

Butch's Rule #31
Always Practice Good Manners

There is nothing you can say that expresses more about you then how much you practice good manners, or good etiquette. When you say "thank you", 'you're welcome", "please", "yes sir", "yes ma'am", etc. What it says to people is that you appear to be a polite person, that you seem to be a person of good character, that you are civil, and, perhaps, that you have class in how you carry yourself.

Conversely, if you do not practice good manners, to the contrary, it may say that you are impolite, perhaps, rude, uncouth, and lacking in class in how you carry yourself. So, the take away is, if you are lacking in the practice of good manners, it is suggested that you work toward improving yourself in this area. The payoff is immeasurable in how, and what, people may think about the kind of person that you are.

Short Illustration:

After a job interview, the candidate sent a thank-you note, used "please" and "thank you" thoughout the process, and maintained a respectful demeanor. The hiring manager was impressed, noting that the candidate's good manners signaled a person of good character and civility.

Butch's Rule #32

The Anti-Discrimination Rule

In the face of discrimination, and persecution, base on race, gender, ethnicity or religion, you should do two things, 1) always speak out, protest, march, vote and fight for what is right, which is fairness, equality, equal treatment, and the dignity of all on an equal basis, and, 2) At the same time, you should simultaneously continue to not be discouraged, and keep working hard, and continue to pursue your goals, and dreams. You can, and should, do both things at the same time, for, if, and when, you do succeed in winning your fight against unfair discrimination, you definitely want to be ready to take advantage of the openings and new opportunities that you fought hard to win.

Short Illustration:

When a local housing board created a discrimintory policy, a group of citizens not only marched and spoke out against it for fairness, but they also simultaneously kept working hard to complete their specialized trading. When the policy was overturned, they were immediately ready to take advantage of the new opportunities they had fought for.

Butch's Rule #33

National Healthcare is a Pact

The concept of National Healthcare is a pact. It is a moral agreement, and commitment, between all of us as citizens of our country that we should have a healthcare system we will collectively contribute to that will be there for all of us as citizen of our country. This should not be looked at as a right, or just another government program, but a universal healthcare system for all of us bound by a deeper moral agreement to be there for each other when medical care and the pursuit of wellness is needed or required. It is not a choice or optional to opt-in or out of something which is a necessity of life and well-being. We all need it. We all will use it. We should all embrace it as a pact between all our citizens. Again, a national healthcare system to be there for all of us as citizens of our country.

Short Illustration:

During a community debate, a speaker argued that funding for a universal health system should be viewed as a moral agreement and commitment--a--pact--where all citizens contribute so that the system is there for all of us when medical care is inevitably needed.

Butch's Rule #34

The Employee Mutual Company (EMC)

A democratically run company, one employee, one vote. In business, there are three (3) basic forms of ownership, or business, 1) sole proprietorship, 2) Partnership, and 3) corporate. I think it is time for the invention of another, the Employee Mutual Company (EMC). With the first three (3) forms of business there is separation between the goals and motivations of management and the goals of employees, (a) management runs the company and is paid a high multiple of the average employee of the company and receives additional perks, sometimes including stock options, and (b) the hired employees gets a competitive salary and employee benefits. In the traditional business forms, companies are setup like a dictatorships where most of the profits go to the owners and senior management which is understandable in a capitalistic system. In an Employee Mutual Company, all employs are treated like owners, and, thereby, is entitled to participation in the selection, and election, of the senior management and is eligible for a share of company profits. I think this a far superior form of business than the other traditional forms of business because everyone is treated and respected equally, and their interested are aligned to work together for the short and long-term success of the company to everyone's mutual benefit. There is less tension between line employees and management because both want the same thing, the mutual success for everyone employed by the company.

(continued on next page)

Short Illustration:

At "InnovationCo" an employee mutual company, a major investment decision was put to a company-wide vote, where every employee had a vote. This democratic process, where all employees were treated like owners, meant the goals of management and the line staff are mutually aligned for the company's success.

Butch's Rule #35

It's Better to be a Reader than a Non-Reader

"I was once was blind and I now I see". When you read, books, newspapers, etc., what you once did not understand before you now have a better understanding. You are better informed and look at things differently. It makes you smarter, better informed, and your social circle looks at you with greater esteem.

Short Illustration:

John, an avid reader, read books and articles about global economics. When discussing the stock market with his friends, he was able to provided informed insight and look at the issues differently, demonstating how reading had made him better informed and earned him greater esteem in his social circle.

CONCLUSION

This book is not meant to be the final word on anything, or give best answers to questions, but to be part of continued thought, and decision making on past ideas. It is up to you to take the torch and carry it forward to continue to improve on past ideas, decisions, thoughts, and thinking. Additionally, when you make further breakthroughs in past ideas, I hope you are generous enough to sharing them with your friends, associates, and the world.

APPENDIX (How to use this book)

This book is not meant to be the final word on anything, or give the best answers to all questions, but to be part of a continuing thinking, and decision making on past, present and future ideas. It is up to you to take the torch and carry it forward to continue to improve on past, present and future ideas, decisions, thoughts, and thinking. Additionally, when you make further breakthroughs, I hope you are generous enough to sharing them with your friends, associates, and the world.